My First Book About DINOSAURS

Donald M. Silver

and

Patricia J. Wynne

Dover Publications, Inc.

Garden City, New York

D1451643

*For Dover Publications' founding genius ... Hayward Cirker,
who brought back to life out-of-print science, art, math,
history, literature, music, and children's books
at a price just about all readers could afford,
and who hired us to create our first book about dinosaurs.*

Enormous and towering over the Earth, or small and close to the ground, the amazing dinosaurs continue to thrill and fascinate us. These incredible creatures roamed our planet millions of years ago, and even though we may see models in museums, we don't really know what they looked like—scientists construct these models using the dinosaurs' fossils as clues. The illustrations in this book will take you on a fascinating journey to the Paleozoic, Mesozoic, and Cenozoic eras, as you glimpse Allosaurus, Megalosaurus, Stegosaurus, Triceratops, Tyrannosaurus rex, Velociraptor, and the birdlike Archaeopteryx, among many others. You'll learn about the dinosaurs' size and physical features, as well as what they ate and where they lived. And you can color each of the illustrations using colored pencils, crayons, or markers.

Copyright
Copyright © 2021 by Dover Publications, Inc.
All rights reserved.

Bibliographical Note
My First Book About Dinosaurs is a new work, first published by
Dover Publications, Inc., in 2021.

International Standard Book Number
ISBN-13: 978-0-486-84556-2
ISBN-10: 0-486-84556-7

Manufactured in the United States by LSC Communications
84556701
www.doverpublications.com
2 4 6 8 10 9 7 5 3 1
2021

A WORLD OF DINOSAURS
Come explore the world of dinosaurs! Along the way expect to find fantastic creatures with bone-crushing teeth, spiked tails, slashing claws, head crests, and even feathers. There will be moving continents, climate changes, and an asteroid crashing into Earth.

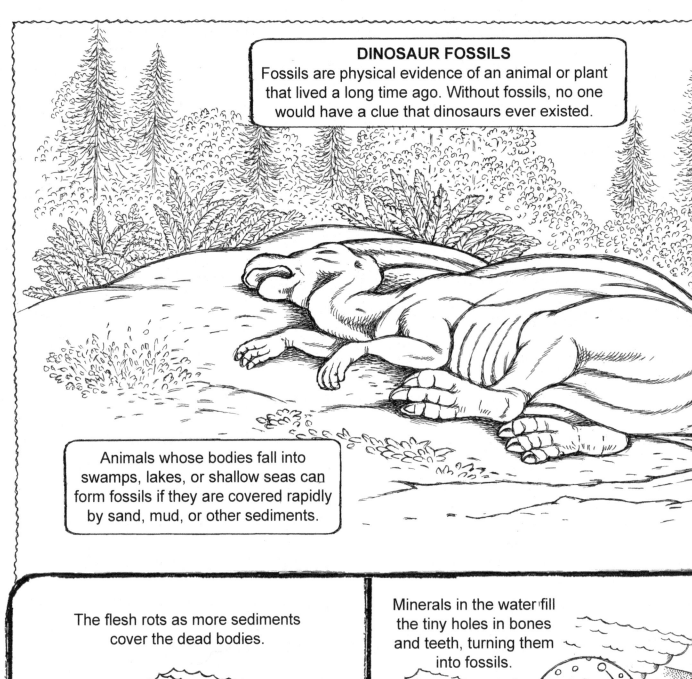

DINOSAUR FOSSILS
Fossils are physical evidence of an animal or plant that lived a long time ago. Without fossils, no one would have a clue that dinosaurs ever existed.

Animals whose bodies fall into swamps, lakes, or shallow seas can form fossils if they are covered rapidly by sand, mud, or other sediments.

The flesh rots as more sediments cover the dead bodies.

Minerals in the water fill the tiny holes in bones and teeth, turning them into fossils.

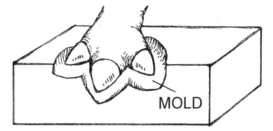

Sometimes a dinosaur footprint in mud formed an impression, called a mold, of the track.

The mold was covered by water, and layers of sediment filled it. Over time, the layers hardened into sedimentary rock.

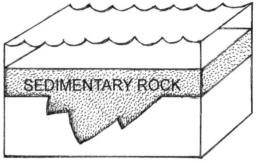

The rock that filled the footprint is called a cast, because it is a stone copy of the dinosaur's track.

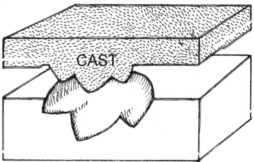

When swamps, lakes, and shallow seas dry up, the sedimentary rock once underwater becomes land.

Under pressure, the layers of sediments turn into sedimentary rock that surrounds the fossils.

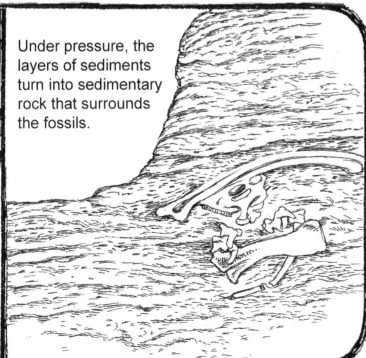

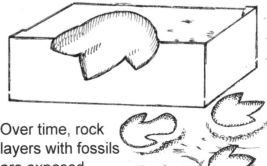

Over time, rock layers with fossils are exposed.

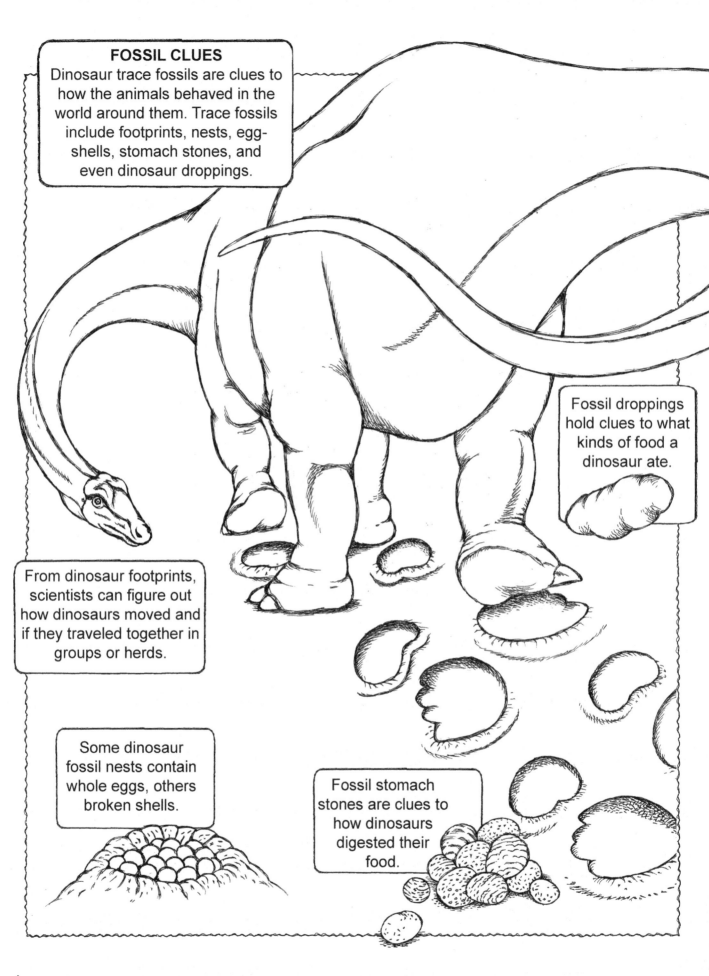

FOSSIL CLUES
Dinosaur trace fossils are clues to how the animals behaved in the world around them. Trace fossils include footprints, nests, egg-shells, stomach stones, and even dinosaur droppings.

Fossil droppings hold clues to what kinds of food a dinosaur ate.

From dinosaur footprints, scientists can figure out how dinosaurs moved and if they traveled together in groups or herds.

Some dinosaur fossil nests contain whole eggs, others broken shells.

Fossil stomach stones are clues to how dinosaurs digested their food.

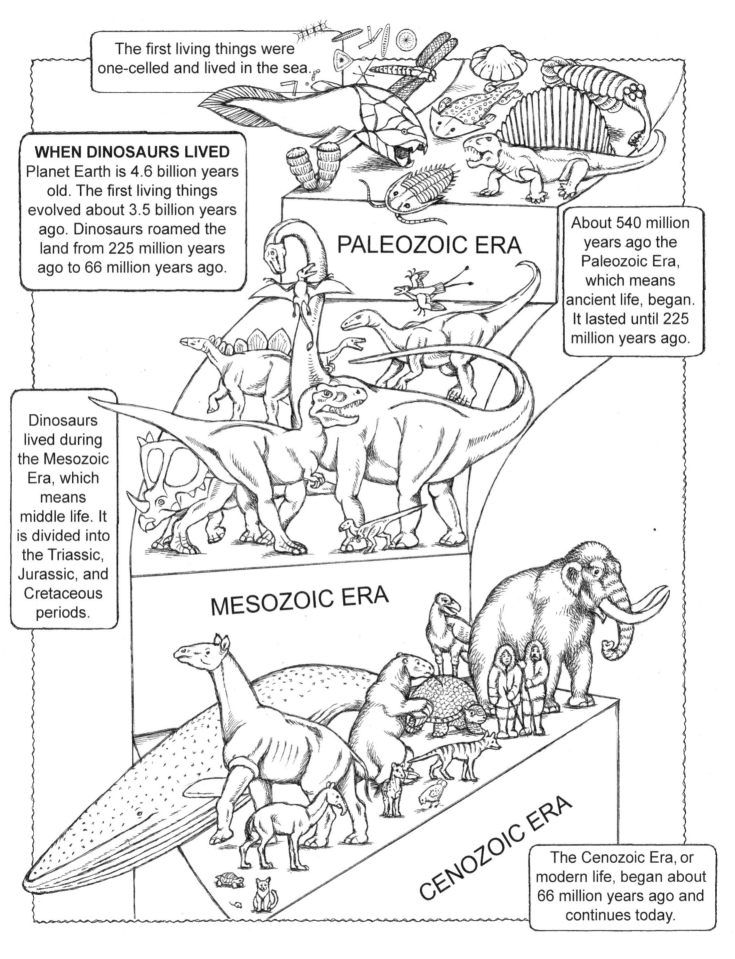

The first living things were one-celled and lived in the sea.

WHEN DINOSAURS LIVED
Planet Earth is 4.6 billion years old. The first living things evolved about 3.5 billion years ago. Dinosaurs roamed the land from 225 million years ago to 66 million years ago.

About 540 million years ago the Paleozoic Era, which means ancient life, began. It lasted until 225 million years ago.

PALEOZOIC ERA

Dinosaurs lived during the Mesozoic Era, which means middle life. It is divided into the Triassic, Jurassic, and Cretaceous periods.

MESOZOIC ERA

CENOZOIC ERA

The Cenozoic Era, or modern life, began about 66 million years ago and continues today.

5

FINDING FOSSILS
Anyone may be lucky enough to find dinosaur fossils. But only trained fossil experts, called paleontologists, know what to do next.

Before removing a fossil, permission must be obtained from the owner of the land on which it was found.

Special tools must be used to carefully dig out fossils without damaging them.

Each fossil is cleaned, covered in padding, and then wrapped in plaster that hardens into a jacket.

Another scientist records where each fossil was found at the dig site.

When fossils arrive at a museum, a skilled "preparator" frees each from its jacket and cleans it for studying.

REBUILDING A DINOSAUR
Rebuilding a dinosaur from its fossil takes a paleontologist to figure out where each bone goes and an artist to reconstruct what the animal looked like.

CHAS R. KNIGHT

EXISTING FOSSIL BONES

XENOCERATOP

Charles Knight's famous dinosaur reconstructions reflect his understanding of animal muscles and bones.

If only a few fossil bones exist, the artist rebuilds the dinosaur based on what is known about closely related dinosaurs.

TRICERATOPS

PLANTS OF THE CRETACEOUS

To reconstruct what a dinosaur looked like, artists research living animal anatomy, habitats, colors and patterns, and coverings such as feathers or scales.

7

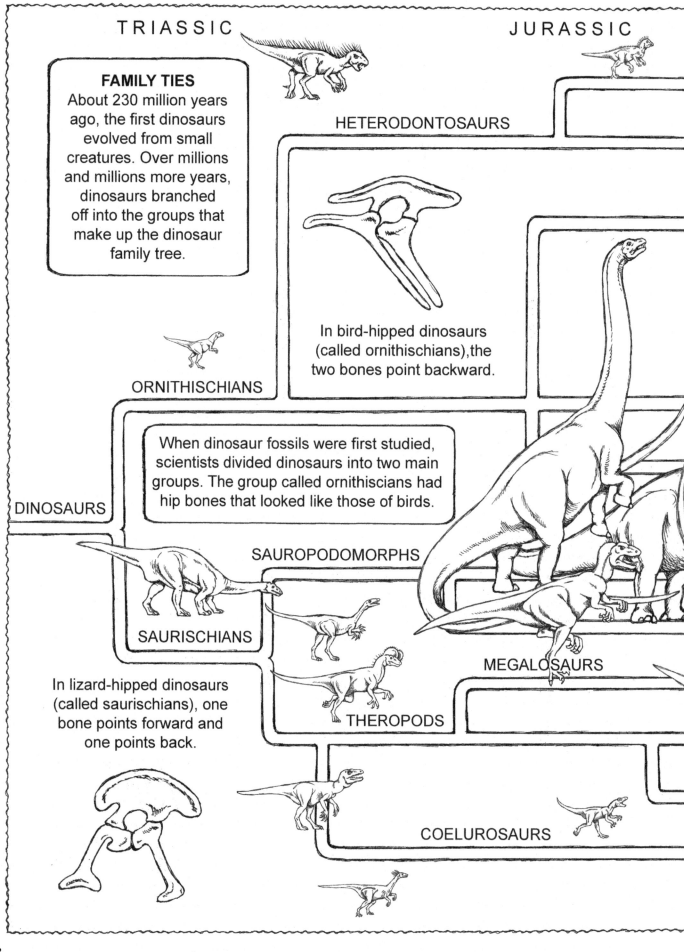

FAMILY TIES

About 230 million years ago, the first dinosaurs evolved from small creatures. Over millions and millions more years, dinosaurs branched off into the groups that make up the dinosaur family tree.

HETERODONTOSAURS

In bird-hipped dinosaurs (called ornithischians), the two bones point backward.

ORNITHISCHIANS

When dinosaur fossils were first studied, scientists divided dinosaurs into two main groups. The group called ornithiscians had hip bones that looked like those of birds.

DINOSAURS

SAUROPODOMORPHS

SAURISCHIANS

MEGALOSAURS

THEROPODS

In lizard-hipped dinosaurs (called saurischians), one bone points forward and one points back.

COELUROSAURS

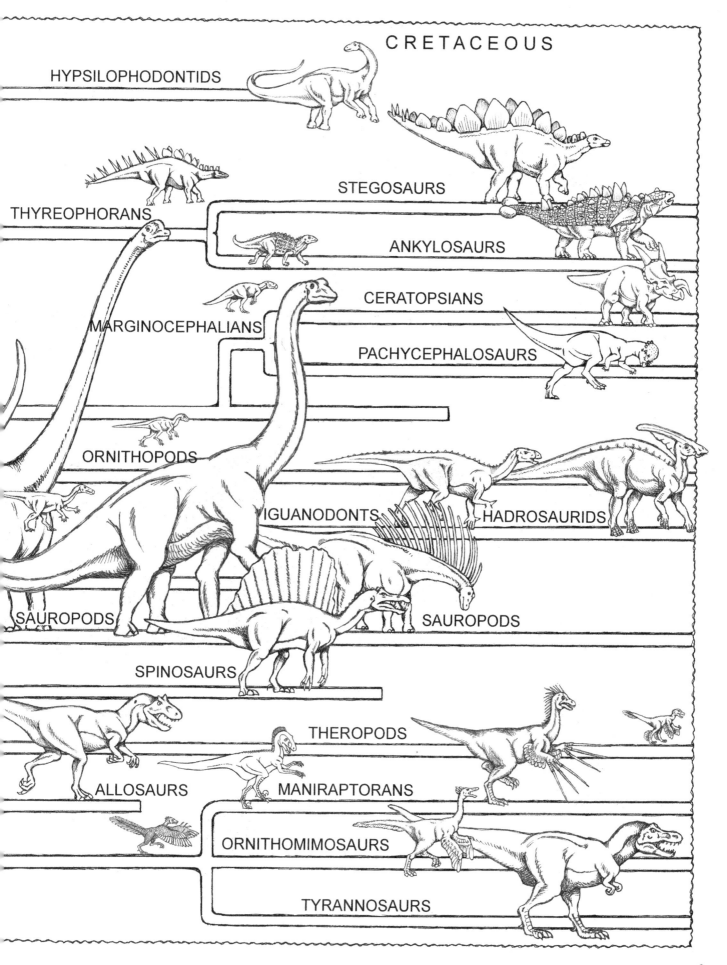

CRETACEOUS

HYPSILOPHODONTIDS

STEGOSAURS

THYREOPHORANS

ANKYLOSAURS

CERATOPSIANS

MARGINOCEPHALIANS

PACHYCEPHALOSAURS

ORNITHOPODS

IGUANODONTS

HADROSAURIDS

SAUROPODS

SAUROPODS

SPINOSAURS

THEROPODS

ALLOSAURS

MANIRAPTORANS

ORNITHOMIMOSAURS

TYRANNOSAURS

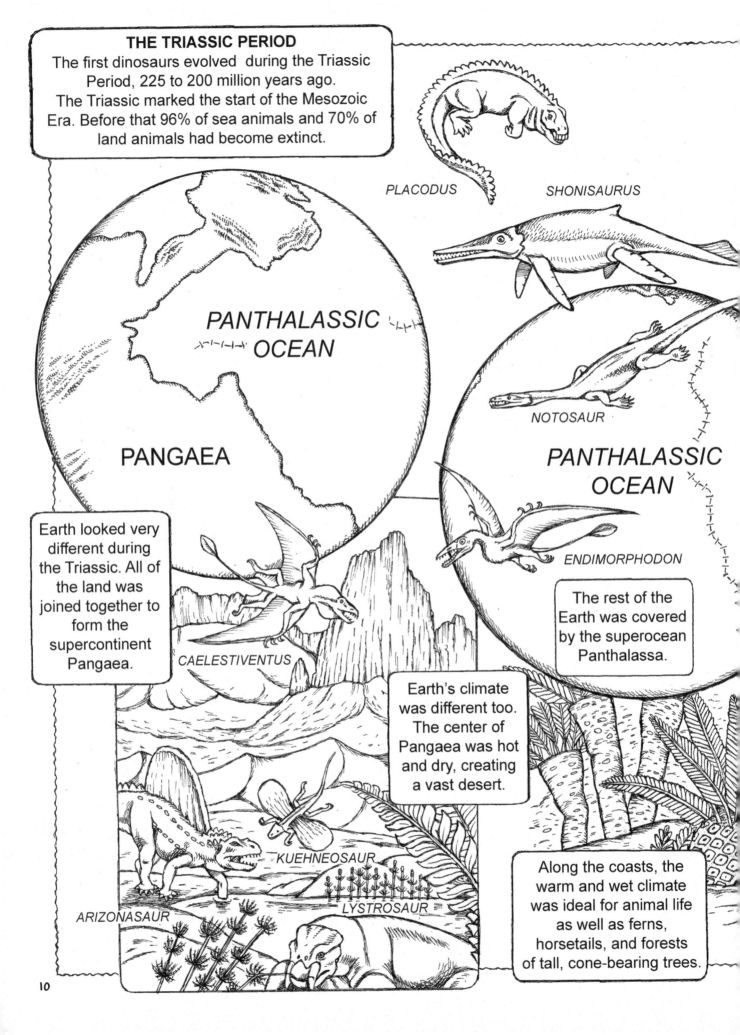

THE TRIASSIC PERIOD
The first dinosaurs evolved during the Triassic Period, 225 to 200 million years ago.
The Triassic marked the start of the Mesozoic Era. Before that 96% of sea animals and 70% of land animals had become extinct.

PLACODUS

SHONISAURUS

PANTHALASSIC OCEAN

NOTOSAUR

PANGAEA

PANTHALASSIC OCEAN

Earth looked very different during the Triassic. All of the land was joined together to form the supercontinent Pangaea.

ENDIMORPHODON

The rest of the Earth was covered by the superocean Panthalassa.

CAELESTIVENTUS

Earth's climate was different too. The center of Pangaea was hot and dry, creating a vast desert.

KUEHNEOSAUR

LYSTROSAUR

ARIZONASAUR

Along the coasts, the warm and wet climate was ideal for animal life as well as ferns, horsetails, and forests of tall, cone-bearing trees.

Around 240 million years ago the first dinosaurs roamed the land. They were often small creatures that walked on their hind legs. Archosaurs like the giant Postosuchus preyed on them.

PLATEOSAURUS

COELOPHYSIS

EOZOSTRODON

LILIENSTEVNUS

CYNOGNATHUS

PLACERIAS

POSTOSUCHUS

OLIGOKYPHUS

EORAPTOR

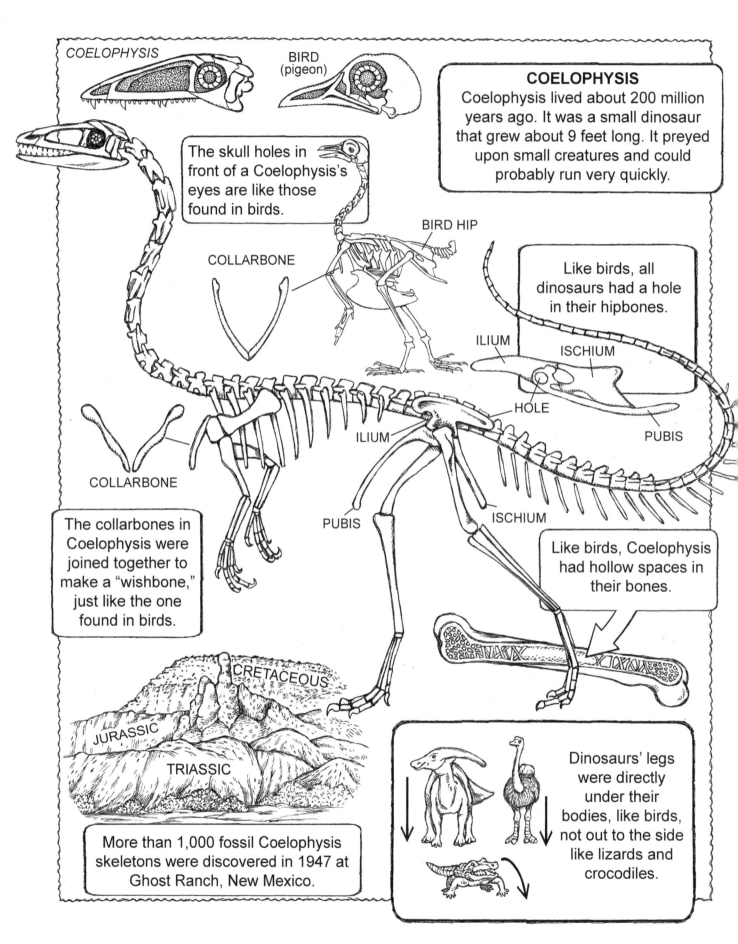

COELOPHYSIS

BIRD (pigeon)

The skull holes in front of a Coelophysis's eyes are like those found in birds.

COELOPHYSIS
Coelophysis lived about 200 million years ago. It was a small dinosaur that grew about 9 feet long. It preyed upon small creatures and could probably run very quickly.

BIRD HIP

COLLARBONE

Like birds, all dinosaurs had a hole in their hipbones.

ILIUM

ISCHIUM

HOLE

PUBIS

ILIUM

COLLARBONE

PUBIS

ISCHIUM

The collarbones in Coelophysis were joined together to make a "wishbone," just like the one found in birds.

Like birds, Coelophysis had hollow spaces in their bones.

CRETACEOUS

JURASSIC

TRIASSIC

Dinosaurs' legs were directly under their bodies, like birds, not out to the side like lizards and crocodiles.

More than 1,000 fossil Coelophysis skeletons were discovered in 1947 at Ghost Ranch, New Mexico.

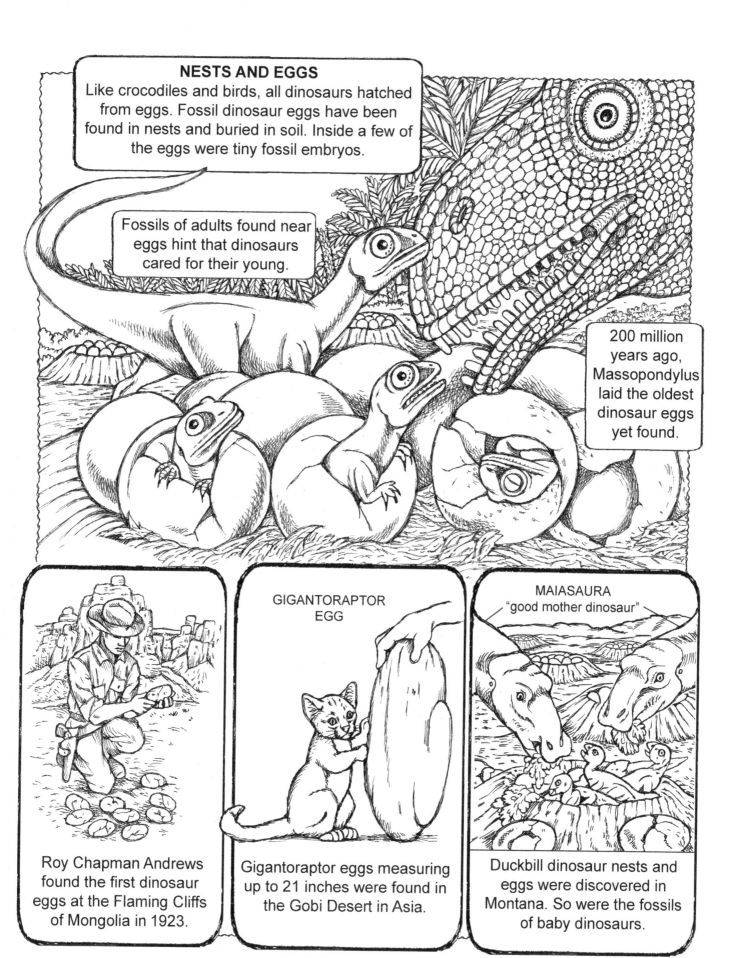

NESTS AND EGGS
Like crocodiles and birds, all dinosaurs hatched from eggs. Fossil dinosaur eggs have been found in nests and buried in soil. Inside a few of the eggs were tiny fossil embryos.

Fossils of adults found near eggs hint that dinosaurs cared for their young.

200 million years ago, Massopondylus laid the oldest dinosaur eggs yet found.

Roy Chapman Andrews found the first dinosaur eggs at the Flaming Cliffs of Mongolia in 1923.

GIGANTORAPTOR EGG

Gigantoraptor eggs measuring up to 21 inches were found in the Gobi Desert in Asia.

MAIASAURA
"good mother dinosaur"

Duckbill dinosaur nests and eggs were discovered in Montana. So were the fossils of baby dinosaurs.

13

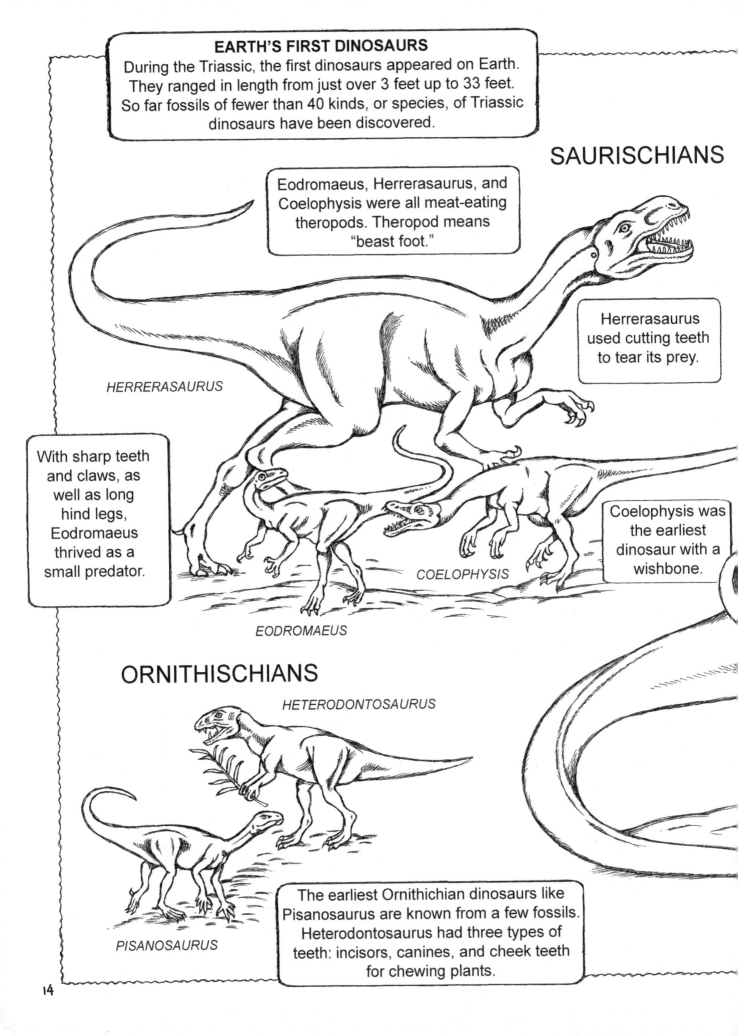

EARTH'S FIRST DINOSAURS
During the Triassic, the first dinosaurs appeared on Earth.
They ranged in length from just over 3 feet up to 33 feet.
So far fossils of fewer than 40 kinds, or species, of Triassic
dinosaurs have been discovered.

SAURISCHIANS

Eodromaeus, Herrerasaurus, and
Coelophysis were all meat-eating
theropods. Theropod means
"beast foot."

Herrerasaurus
used cutting teeth
to tear its prey.

HERRERASAURUS

With sharp teeth
and claws, as
well as long
hind legs,
Eodromaeus
thrived as a
small predator.

Coelophysis was
the earliest
dinosaur with a
wishbone.

COELOPHYSIS

EODROMAEUS

ORNITHISCHIANS

HETERODONTOSAURUS

The earliest Ornithichian dinosaurs like
Pisanosaurus are known from a few fossils.
Heterodontosaurus had three types of
teeth: incisors, canines, and cheek teeth
for chewing plants.

PISANOSAURUS

A Plateosaurus's large thumb could have been used to slice plants to eat. At 30 feet long it was one of the largest Triassic dinosaurs.

Thecodontoaurus, Plateosaurus, and Blikanasaurus were sauropodomorphs. Sauropodomorphs and theropods are the two types of saurischians.

PLATEOSAURUS

Blikanasaurus could be the earliest dinosaur to walk on four legs.

BLIKANASAURUS

THECODONTOSAURUS

Plant-eating Thecodontosaurus was the fourth dinosaur to be named.

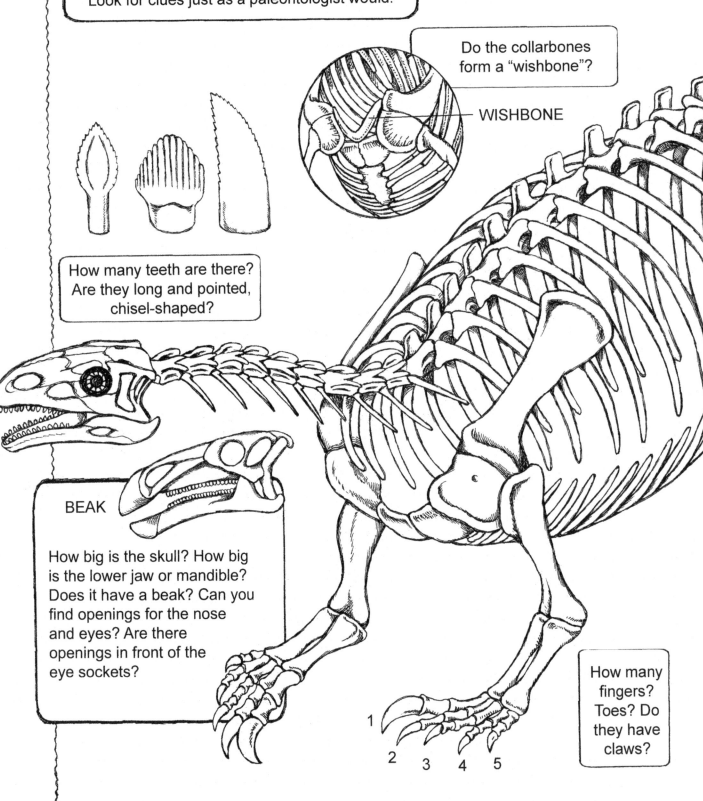

LOOK CLOSELY
Dinosaur skeletons hold clues to the ways in which different dinosaurs lived. Next time you are at a natural history museum with dinosaur displays, take a close look at each skeleton. Look for clues just as a paleontologist would.

How many ribs are there?

Do the collarbones form a "wishbone"?

WISHBONE

How many teeth are there? Are they long and pointed, chisel-shaped?

BEAK

How big is the skull? How big is the lower jaw or mandible? Does it have a beak? Can you find openings for the nose and eyes? Are there openings in front of the eye sockets?

1
2   3   4   5

How many fingers? Toes? Do they have claws?

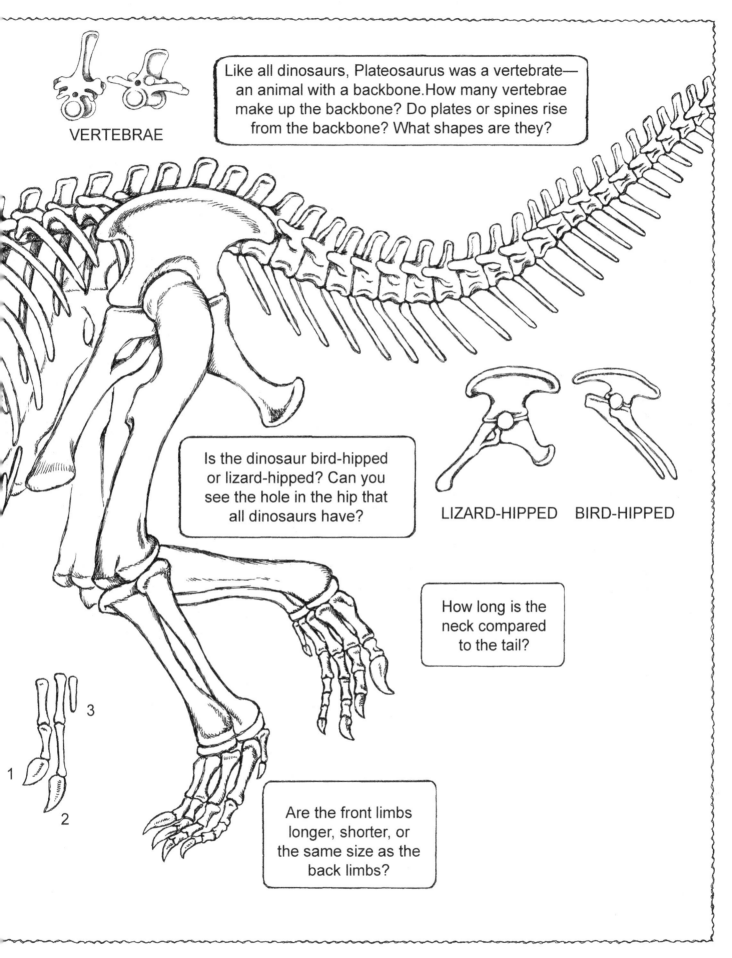

VERTEBRAE

Like all dinosaurs, Plateosaurus was a vertebrate—
an animal with a backbone. How many vertebrae
make up the backbone? Do plates or spines rise
from the backbone? What shapes are they?

Is the dinosaur bird-hipped
or lizard-hipped? Can you
see the hole in the hip that
all dinosaurs have?

LIZARD-HIPPED   BIRD-HIPPED

How long is the
neck compared
to the tail?

3

1

2

Are the front limbs
longer, shorter, or
the same size as the
back limbs?

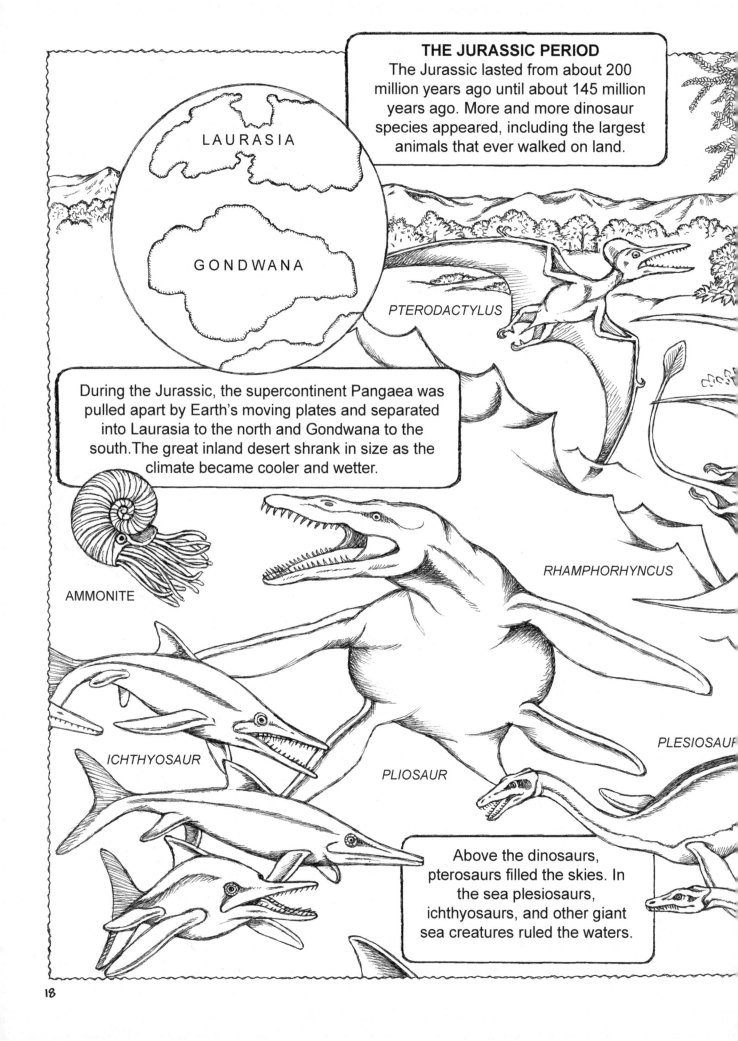

THE JURASSIC PERIOD
The Jurassic lasted from about 200 million years ago until about 145 million years ago. More and more dinosaur species appeared, including the largest animals that ever walked on land.

LAURASIA

GONDWANA

PTERODACTYLUS

During the Jurassic, the supercontinent Pangaea was pulled apart by Earth's moving plates and separated into Laurasia to the north and Gondwana to the south. The great inland desert shrank in size as the climate became cooler and wetter.

RHAMPHORHYNCUS

AMMONITE

PLESIOSAU

ICHTHYOSAUR

PLIOSAUR

Above the dinosaurs, pterosaurs filled the skies. In the sea plesiosaurs, ichthyosaurs, and other giant sea creatures ruled the waters.

STEGOSAURUS

ALLOSAURUS

BRACHIOSAURUS

BRONTOSAURUS

PTERODON

ORNITHOLESTES

GUANLONG

SOLNHOFEN LAGOON

COMPSOGNATHUS

ARCHAEOPTERYX

COMPSOGNATHUS

ICHTHYOSAUR

Lush forests of cone-bearing trees, or conifers, grew across the lands along with ferns, horsetails, and other kinds of plants. In Germany, a lagoon preserved in fossils was found.

JURASSIC MEAT-EATERS
New kinds of meat-eating theropods evolved during the Jurassic. They had knife-sharp teeth, and strong muscles and curved claws on their hands and feet for attacking their prey.

An Allosaurus's razor-sharp teeth had sawlike edges; its thumb claws grew up to 10 inches long. No wonder it was one of the top Jurassic predators.

COMPSOGNATHUS

ALLOSAURUS

With its long legs, Compsognathus could run very fast to catch lizards and insects.

CRYOLOPHOSAUR

Cryolophosaurs lived in what is now Antarctica.

Ornitholestes hunted baby dinosaurs, lizards, and other small creatures. Like birds, it grew feathers.

CERATOSAURUS

ORNITHOLESTES

Ceratosaurus may have used its flexible tail to swim after its dinner.

GUANLONG

Guanlong belongs to the Tyrannosaur group of predatory dinosaurs. Along with scraping teeth and muscular legs, it had a crest on its head.

DILOPHOSAURUS

Dilophosaurus was a top predator in the early Jurassic period.

In 1854, Richard Owens drew Megalosaurus, making it one of the first dinosaurs to be drawn.

MEGALOSAURUS

At about 27 feet long, Megalosaurus was one of the Jurassic's biggest predators. Strong arms and powerful jaws would have been ideal weapons to rip into a Stegosaur.

5 FEET

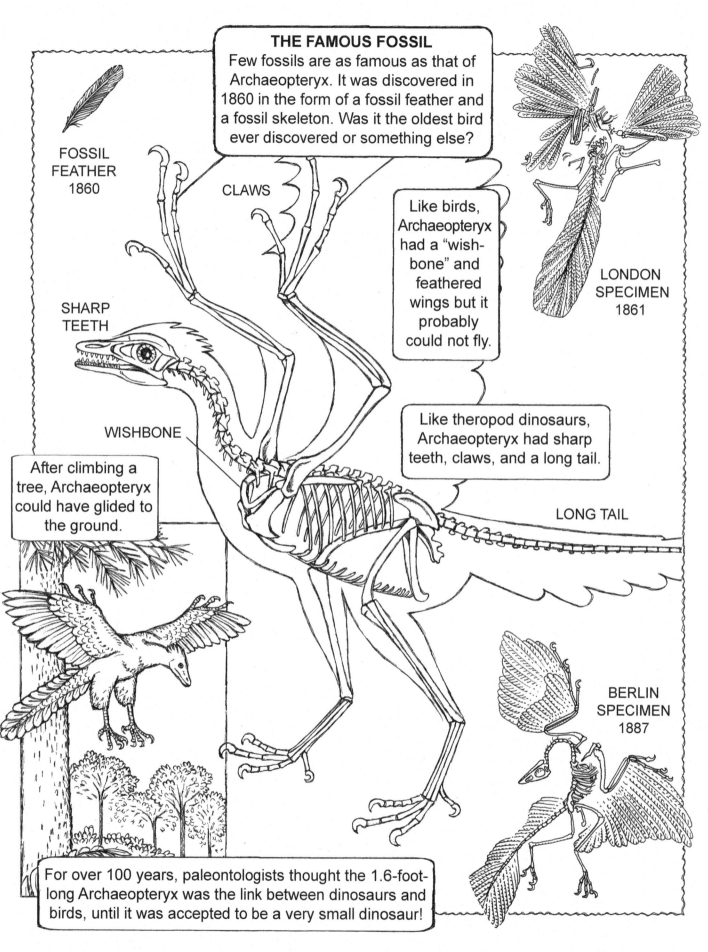

THE FAMOUS FOSSIL
Few fossils are as famous as that of Archaeopteryx. It was discovered in 1860 in the form of a fossil feather and a fossil skeleton. Was it the oldest bird ever discovered or something else?

FOSSIL FEATHER 1860

CLAWS

SHARP TEETH

Like birds, Archaeopteryx had a "wishbone" and feathered wings but it probably could not fly.

LONDON SPECIMEN 1861

WISHBONE

Like theropod dinosaurs, Archaeopteryx had sharp teeth, claws, and a long tail.

LONG TAIL

After climbing a tree, Archaeopteryx could have glided to the ground.

BERLIN SPECIMEN 1887

For over 100 years, paleontologists thought the 1.6-foot-long Archaeopteryx was the link between dinosaurs and birds, until it was accepted to be a very small dinosaur!

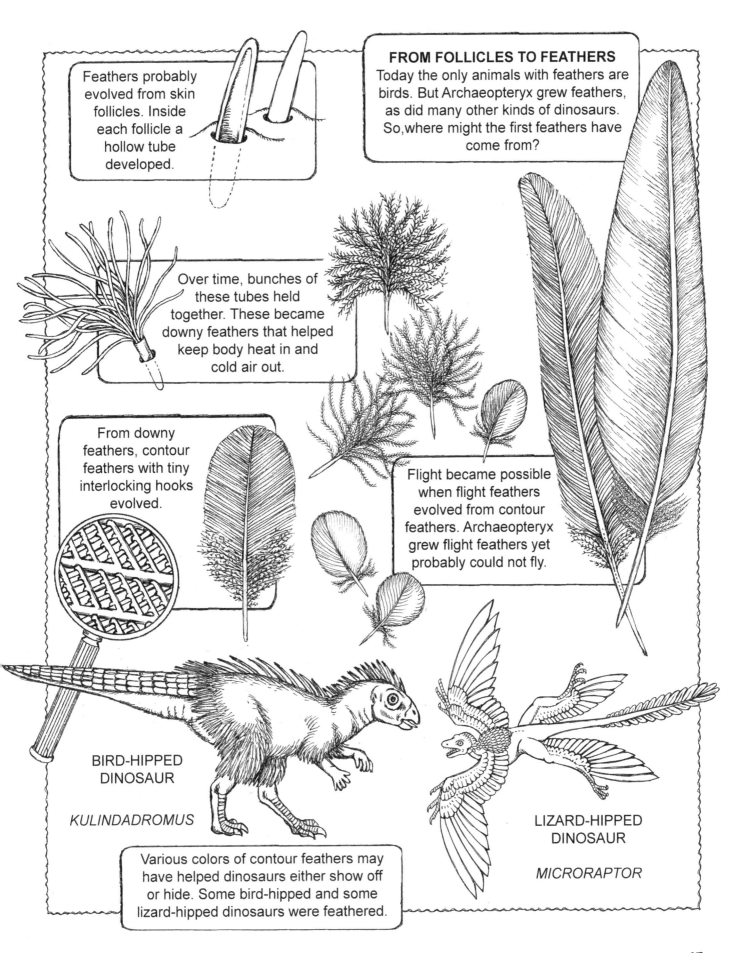

Feathers probably evolved from skin follicles. Inside each follicle a hollow tube developed.

FROM FOLLICLES TO FEATHERS
Today the only animals with feathers are birds. But Archaeopteryx grew feathers, as did many other kinds of dinosaurs. So, where might the first feathers have come from?

Over time, bunches of these tubes held together. These became downy feathers that helped keep body heat in and cold air out.

From downy feathers, contour feathers with tiny interlocking hooks evolved.

Flight became possible when flight feathers evolved from contour feathers. Archaeopteryx grew flight feathers yet probably could not fly.

BIRD-HIPPED DINOSAUR

KULINDADROMUS

LIZARD-HIPPED DINOSAUR

MICRORAPTOR

Various colors of contour feathers may have helped dinosaurs either show off or hide. Some bird-hipped and some lizard-hipped dinosaurs were feathered.

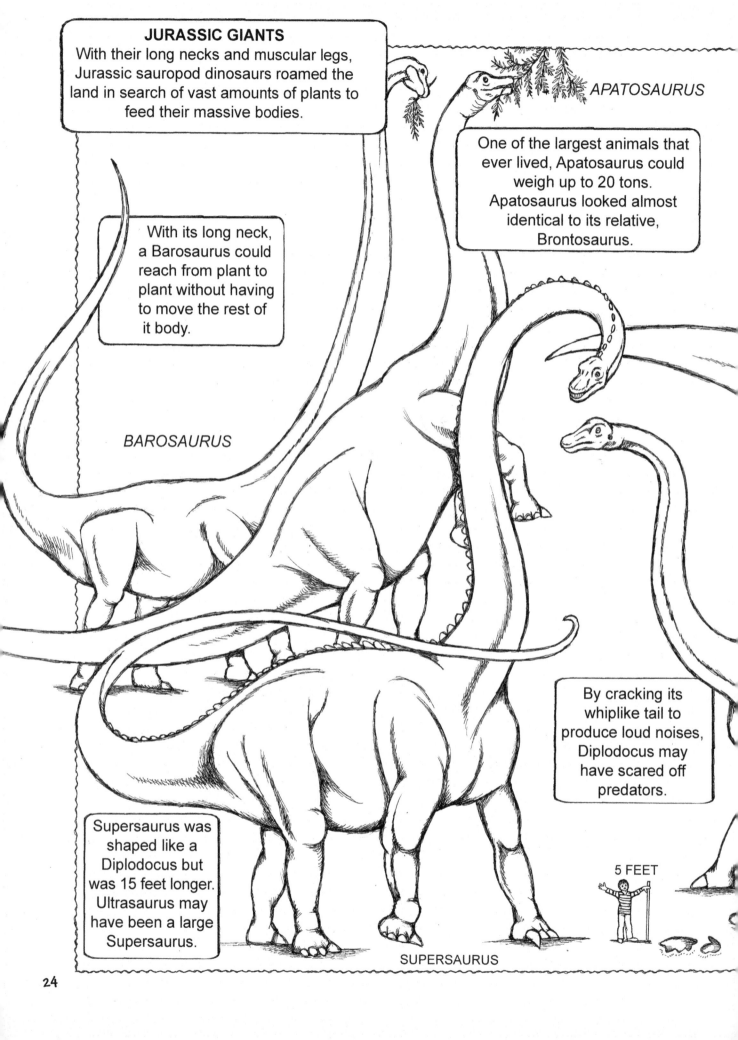

JURASSIC GIANTS
With their long necks and muscular legs, Jurassic sauropod dinosaurs roamed the land in search of vast amounts of plants to feed their massive bodies.

APATOSAURUS

One of the largest animals that ever lived, Apatosaurus could weigh up to 20 tons. Apatosaurus looked almost identical to its relative, Brontosaurus.

With its long neck, a Barosaurus could reach from plant to plant without having to move the rest of it body.

BAROSAURUS

By cracking its whiplike tail to produce loud noises, Diplodocus may have scared off predators.

Supersaurus was shaped like a Diplodocus but was 15 feet longer. Ultrasaurus may have been a large Supersaurus.

5 FEET

SUPERSAURUS

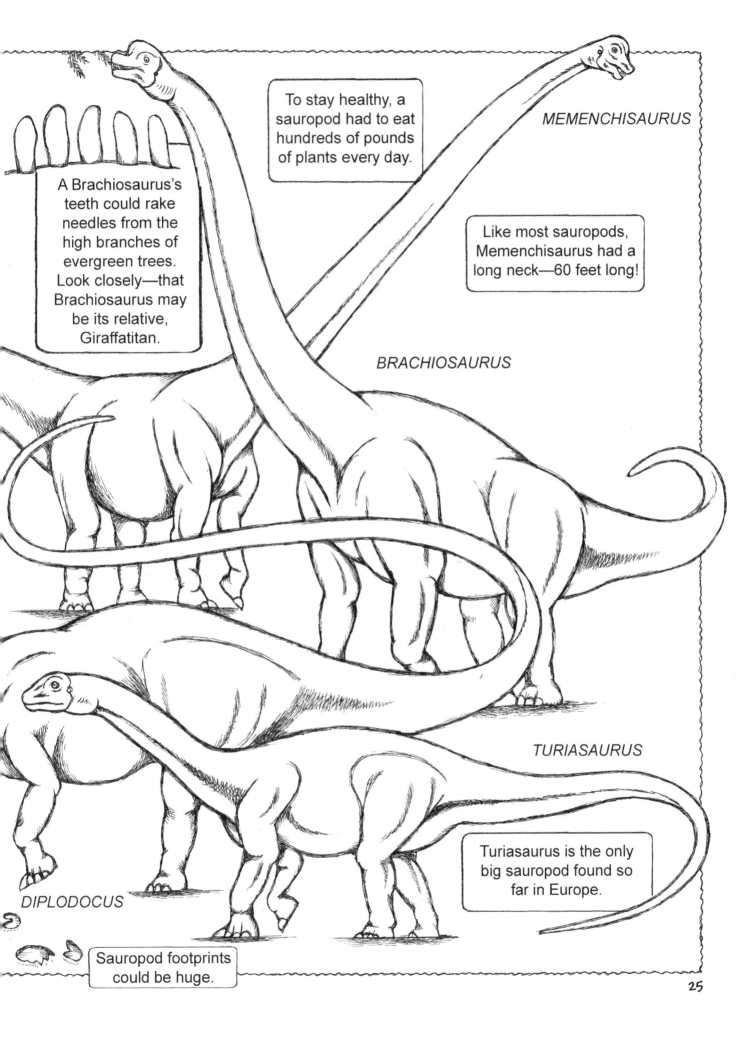

To stay healthy, a sauropod had to eat hundreds of pounds of plants every day.

MEMENCHISAURUS

A Brachiosaurus's teeth could rake needles from the high branches of evergreen trees. Look closely—that Brachiosaurus may be its relative, Giraffatitan.

Like most sauropods, Memenchisaurus had a long neck—60 feet long!

BRACHIOSAURUS

TURIASAURUS

DIPLODOCUS

Turiasaurus is the only big sauropod found so far in Europe.

Sauropod footprints could be huge.

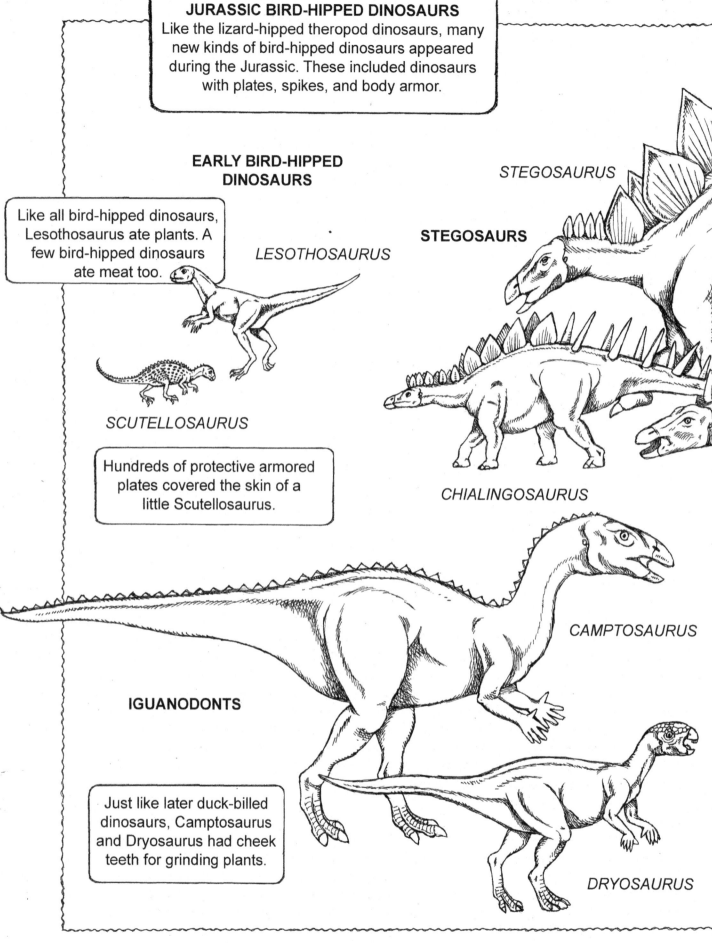

JURASSIC BIRD-HIPPED DINOSAURS
Like the lizard-hipped theropod dinosaurs, many new kinds of bird-hipped dinosaurs appeared during the Jurassic. These included dinosaurs with plates, spikes, and body armor.

EARLY BIRD-HIPPED DINOSAURS

STEGOSAURUS

Like all bird-hipped dinosaurs, Lesothosaurus ate plants. A few bird-hipped dinosaurs ate meat too.

LESOTHOSAURUS

STEGOSAURS

SCUTELLOSAURUS

Hundreds of protective armored plates covered the skin of a little Scutellosaurus.

CHIALINGOSAURUS

CAMPTOSAURUS

IGUANODONTS

Just like later duck-billed dinosaurs, Camptosaurus and Dryosaurus had cheek teeth for grinding plants.

DRYOSAURUS

Bony plates on the Stegosaur's back may have been for temperature control. Its tail spikes could have warned off predators or attracted mates.

FIVE FEET

Like all other bird-hipped dinosaurs, Tuojiangosaurus's jaws were beaked at the front and it chewed its food rather than swallowing it whole.

TUOJIANGOSAURUS

ANKYLOSAURS

These early armored dinosaurs were small compared to their giant Cretaceous descendants.

GARGOYLEOSAURUS

TIANCHISAURUS

MYMOORAPELTA

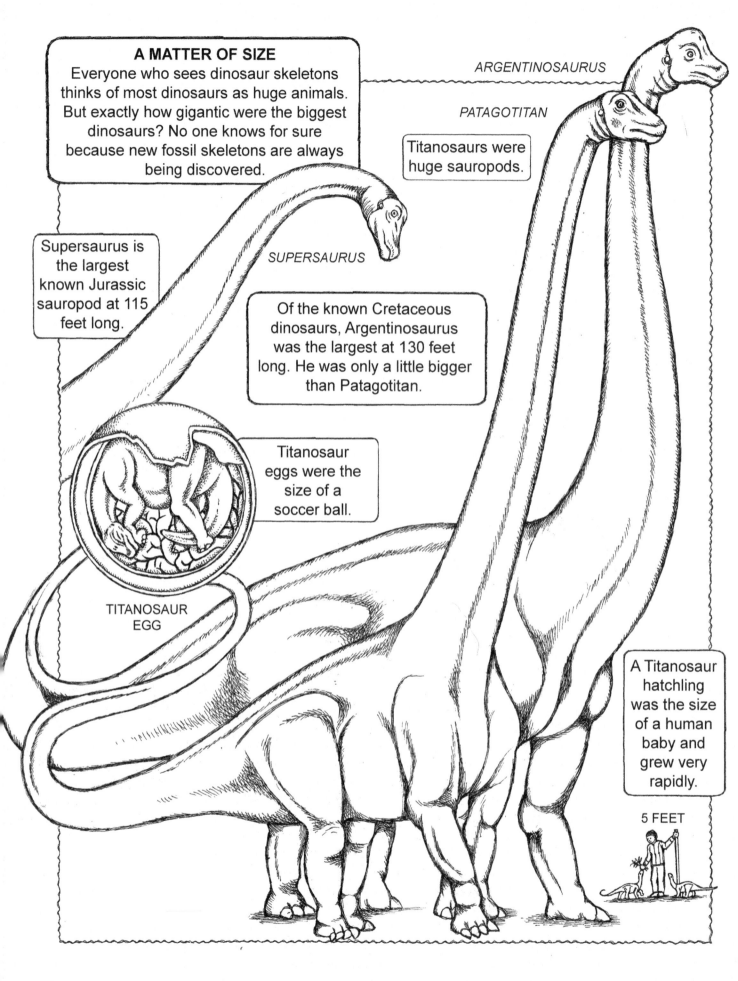

A MATTER OF SIZE
Everyone who sees dinosaur skeletons thinks of most dinosaurs as huge animals. But exactly how gigantic were the biggest dinosaurs? No one knows for sure because new fossil skeletons are always being discovered.

ARGENTINOSAURUS

PATAGOTITAN

Titanosaurs were huge sauropods.

Supersaurus is the largest known Jurassic sauropod at 115 feet long.

SUPERSAURUS

Of the known Cretaceous dinosaurs, Argentinosaurus was the largest at 130 feet long. He was only a little bigger than Patagotitan.

Titanosaur eggs were the size of a soccer ball.

TITANOSAUR EGG

A Titanosaur hatchling was the size of a human baby and grew very rapidly.

5 FEET

SMALL DINOSAURS
Not all dinosaurs were giant-sized. Some of the most interesting dinosaurs were small creatures.

XIAOTINGIA

Xiaotingia is related to Velociraptor.

JURAVENATOR

Found near Archaeopteryx, Juravenator has only one fossil, and it is a juvenile carnivore.

NANOSAURUS

Nanosaurus means "small lizard."

FRUITADENS

Fruitadens, a bird-hipped dinosaur, ate plants and meat.

Tianyulong was covered with fuzzy protofeathers.

TIANYULONG

ARCHAEOPTERYX

Epidexipteryx had the first known ornamental feathers.

Segisaurus is known just from one fossil and had a wishbone.

ONE FOOT

SEGISAURUS

EPIDEXIPTERYX

29

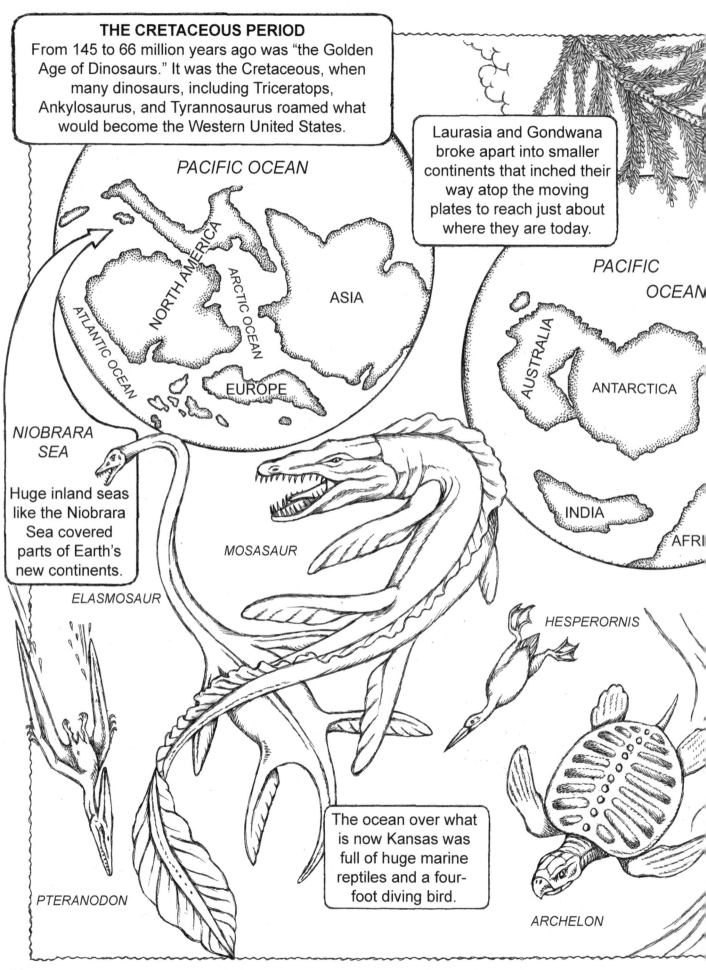

THE CRETACEOUS PERIOD
From 145 to 66 million years ago was "the Golden Age of Dinosaurs." It was the Cretaceous, when many dinosaurs, including Triceratops, Ankylosaurus, and Tyrannosaurus roamed what would become the Western United States.

Laurasia and Gondwana broke apart into smaller continents that inched their way atop the moving plates to reach just about where they are today.

PACIFIC OCEAN

PACIFIC OCEAN

NORTH AMERICA

ARCTIC OCEAN

ATLANTIC OCEAN

ASIA

EUROPE

AUSTRALIA

ANTARCTICA

INDIA

AFRI

NIOBRARA SEA

Huge inland seas like the Niobrara Sea covered parts of Earth's new continents.

ELASMOSAUR

MOSASAUR

HESPERORNIS

The ocean over what is now Kansas was full of huge marine reptiles and a four-foot diving bird.

PTERANODON

ARCHELON

During the Cretaceous, the first flowering plants grew and blossomed on Earth.

Earth's climate stayed warm during much of the Cretaceous. Both the North and South poles were ice-free as a result of the global warming.

SOUTH AMERICA

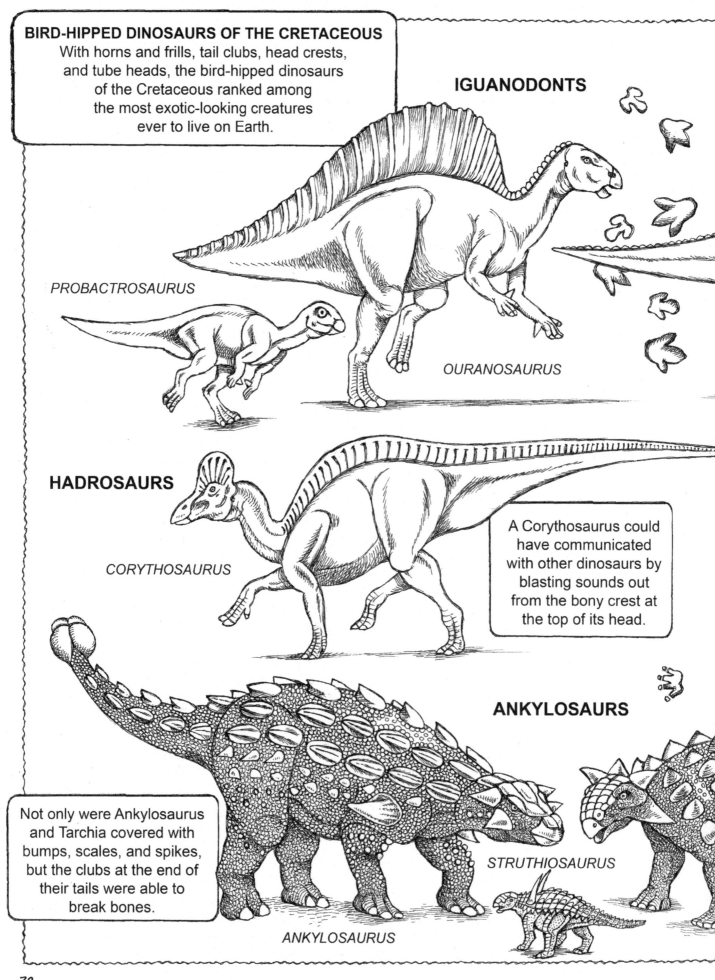

BIRD-HIPPED DINOSAURS OF THE CRETACEOUS
With horns and frills, tail clubs, head crests, and tube heads, the bird-hipped dinosaurs of the Cretaceous ranked among the most exotic-looking creatures ever to live on Earth.

IGUANODONTS

PROBACTROSAURUS

OURANOSAURUS

HADROSAURS

CORYTHOSAURUS

A Corythosaurus could have communicated with other dinosaurs by blasting sounds out from the bony crest at the top of its head.

ANKYLOSAURS

Not only were Ankylosaurus and Tarchia covered with bumps, scales, and spikes, but the clubs at the end of their tails were able to break bones.

STRUTHIOSAURUS

ANKYLOSAURUS

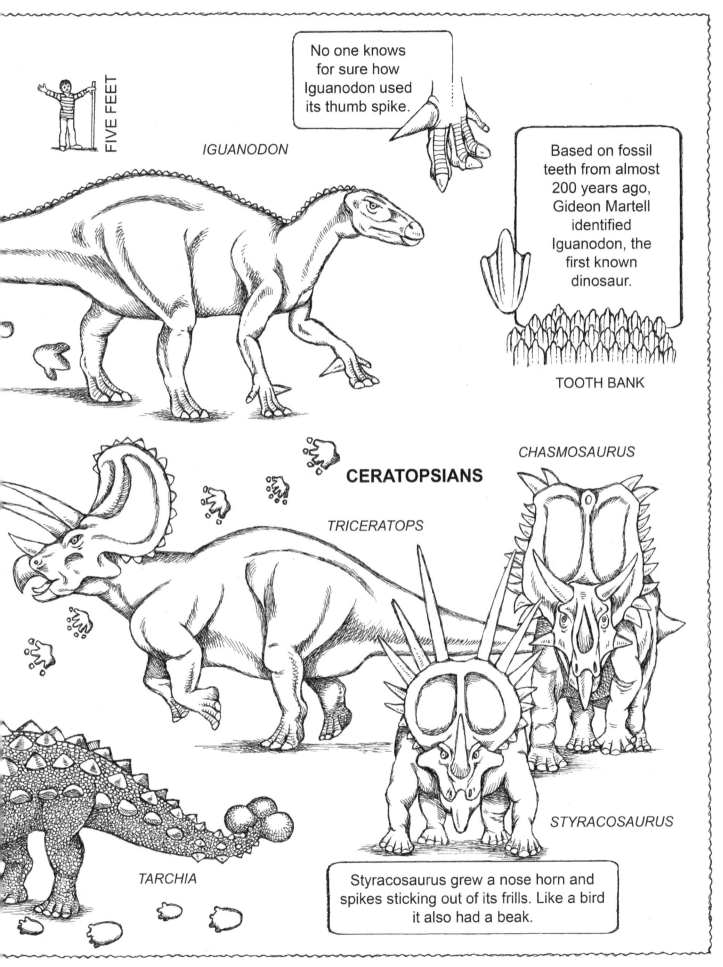

FIVE FEET

No one knows for sure how Iguanodon used its thumb spike.

IGUANODON

Based on fossil teeth from almost 200 years ago, Gideon Martell identified Iguanodon, the first known dinosaur.

TOOTH BANK

CERATOPSIANS

CHASMOSAURUS

TRICERATOPS

STYRACOSAURUS

TARCHIA

Styracosaurus grew a nose horn and spikes sticking out of its frills. Like a bird it also had a beak.

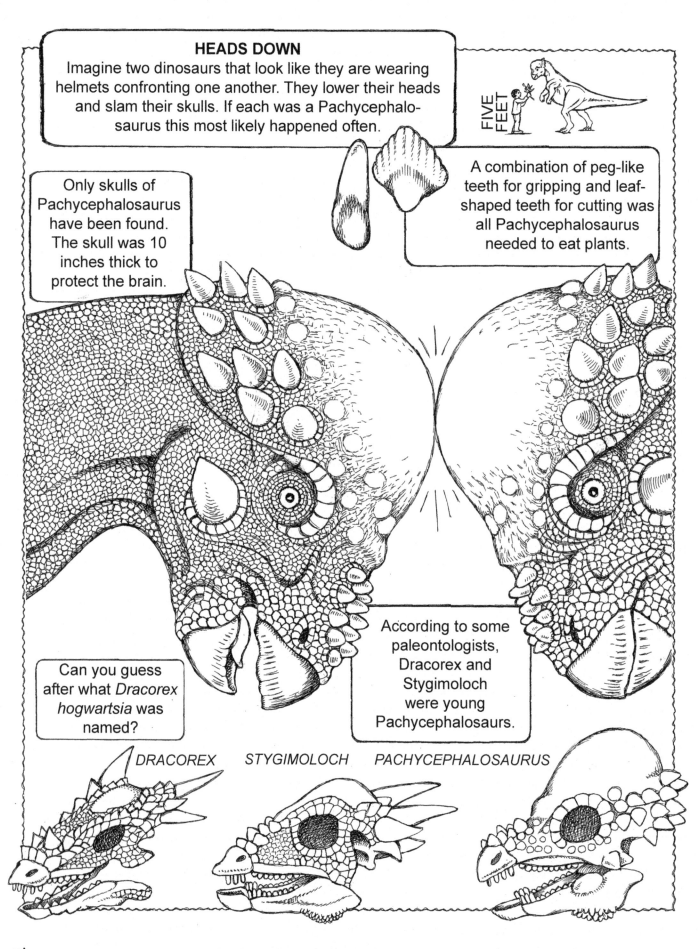

HEADS DOWN
Imagine two dinosaurs that look like they are wearing helmets confronting one another. They lower their heads and slam their skulls. If each was a Pachycephalosaurus this most likely happened often.

FIVE FEET

Only skulls of Pachycephalosaurus have been found. The skull was 10 inches thick to protect the brain.

A combination of peg-like teeth for gripping and leaf-shaped teeth for cutting was all Pachycephalosaurus needed to eat plants.

Can you guess after what *Dracorex hogwartsia* was named?

According to some paleontologists, Dracorex and Stygimoloch were young Pachycephalosaurs.

DRACOREX *STYGIMOLOCH* *PACHYCEPHALOSAURUS*

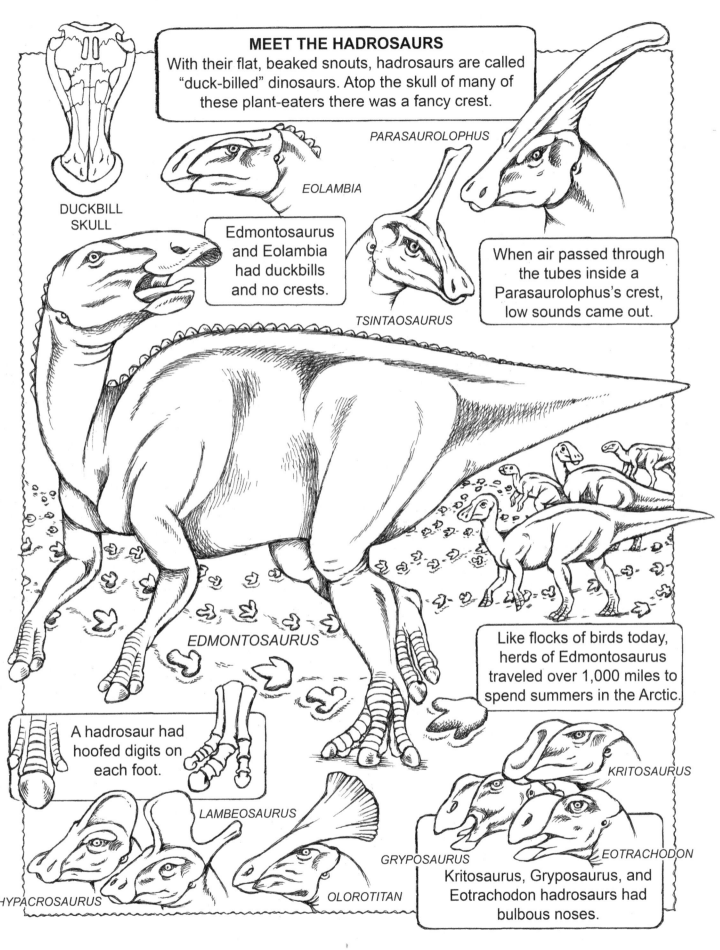

MEET THE HADROSAURS

With their flat, beaked snouts, hadrosaurs are called "duck-billed" dinosaurs. Atop the skull of many of these plant-eaters there was a fancy crest.

DUCKBILL SKULL

EOLAMBIA

PARASAUROLOPHUS

Edmontosaurus and Eolambia had duckbills and no crests.

TSINTAOSAURUS

When air passed through the tubes inside a Parasaurolophus's crest, low sounds came out.

EDMONTOSAURUS

Like flocks of birds today, herds of Edmontosaurus traveled over 1,000 miles to spend summers in the Arctic.

A hadrosaur had hoofed digits on each foot.

LAMBEOSAURUS

HYPACROSAURUS

OLOROTITAN

GRYPOSAURUS

KRITOSAURUS

EOTRACHODON

Kritosaurus, Gryposaurus, and Eotrachodon hadrosaurs had bulbous noses.

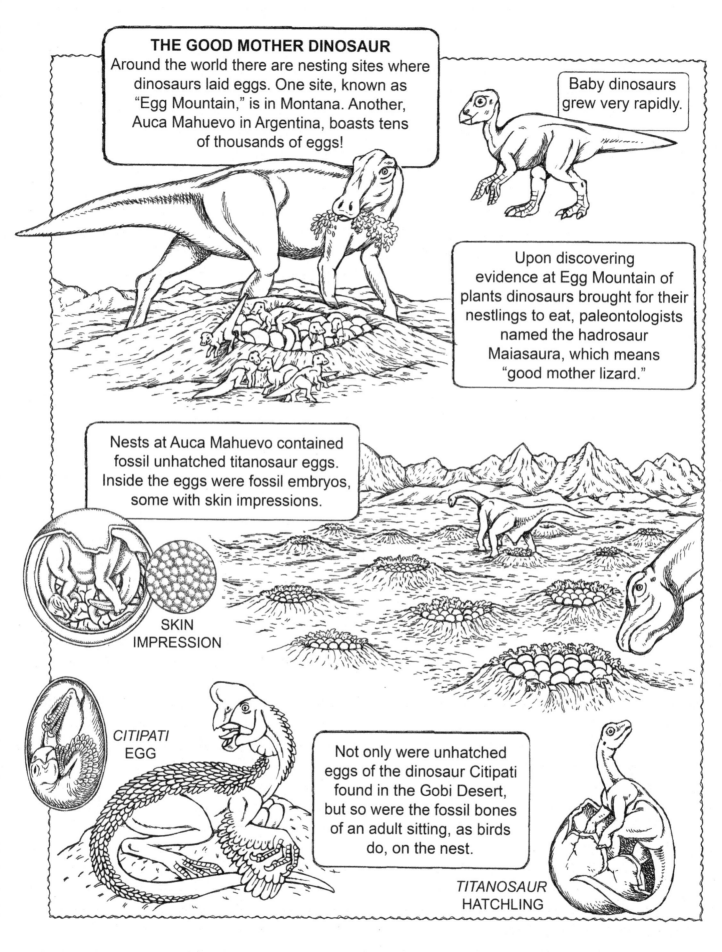

THE GOOD MOTHER DINOSAUR
Around the world there are nesting sites where dinosaurs laid eggs. One site, known as "Egg Mountain," is in Montana. Another, Auca Mahuevo in Argentina, boasts tens of thousands of eggs!

Baby dinosaurs grew very rapidly.

Upon discovering evidence at Egg Mountain of plants dinosaurs brought for their nestlings to eat, paleontologists named the hadrosaur Maiasaura, which means "good mother lizard."

Nests at Auca Mahuevo contained fossil unhatched titanosaur eggs. Inside the eggs were fossil embryos, some with skin impressions.

SKIN IMPRESSION

CITIPATI EGG

Not only were unhatched eggs of the dinosaur Citipati found in the Gobi Desert, but so were the fossil bones of an adult sitting, as birds do, on the nest.

TITANOSAUR HATCHLING

DINOSAURS FROM WAY DOWN UNDER
During the Cretaceous the land that is today Australia and Antarctica was so far south that dinosaurs there lived for months in total darkness inside the Antarctic Circle.

AUSTRALOVENATOR

Kakuru's leg bones are fossilized opal!

KAKURU

SERENDIPACERATOPS

Serendipaceratops was a little relative of Triceratops.

Australovenator's bones were found with those of a sauropod like Wintonotitan. Australovenator was one of the last allosauruses. Was the sauropod its last meal?

AUSTRALIA TODAY

NEW ZEALAND

AUSTRALIA

ANTARCTICA

SOUTH POLE

ANTARCTIC CIRCLE

Timimus was a tiny relative of T. rex.

TIMIMUS

MINMI

Fossil fruit, seeds, and other temperate forest plants were dug up with the fossil bones of Minmi.

WINTONOTITAN

LEAELLYNASAURUS

MUTTABURRASAURUS

Tiny Leaellynasaurus lived in large groups.

The bump on Muttaburrasaurus's nose could have been used to make sounds in the dense, dark forests of Antarctica.

Atlascopcosaurus was a small iguanodon.

FIVE FEET

ATLASCOPCOSAURUS

31

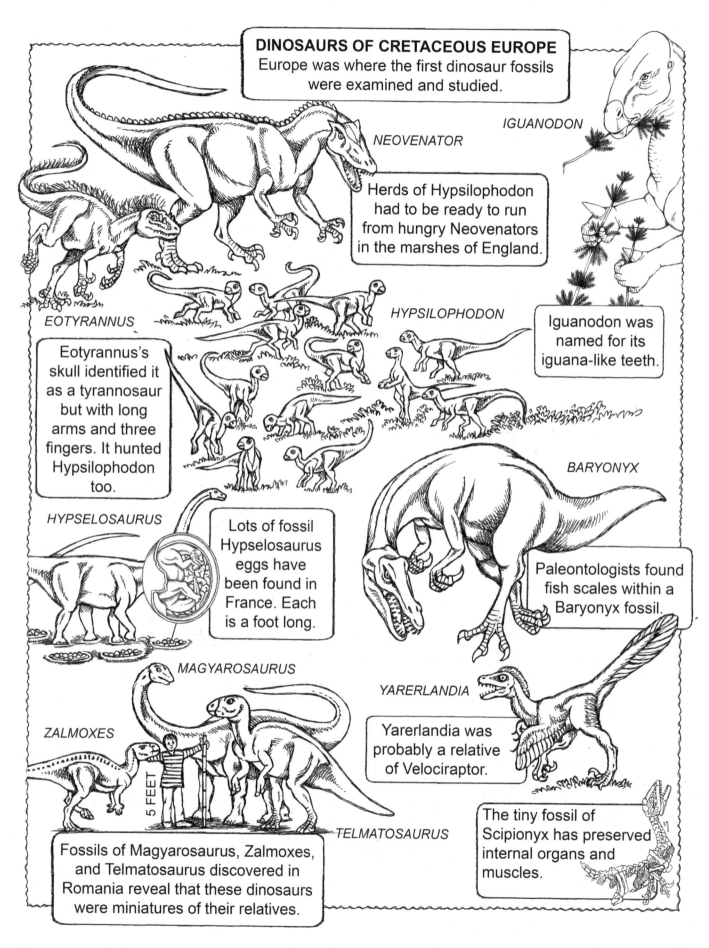

DINOSAURS OF CRETACEOUS EUROPE
Europe was where the first dinosaur fossils were examined and studied.

NEOVENATOR

IGUANODON

Herds of Hypsilophodon had to be ready to run from hungry Neovenators in the marshes of England.

EOTYRANNUS

HYPSILOPHODON

Iguanodon was named for its iguana-like teeth.

Eotyrannus's skull identified it as a tyrannosaur but with long arms and three fingers. It hunted Hypsilophodon too.

BARYONYX

HYPSELOSAURUS

Lots of fossil Hypselosaurus eggs have been found in France. Each is a foot long.

Paleontologists found fish scales within a Baryonyx fossil.

MAGYAROSAURUS

YARERLANDIA

ZALMOXES

5 FEET

Yarerlandia was probably a relative of Velociraptor.

TELMATOSAURUS

Fossils of Magyarosaurus, Zalmoxes, and Telmatosaurus discovered in Romania reveal that these dinosaurs were miniatures of their relatives.

The tiny fossil of Scipionyx has preserved internal organs and muscles.

AFRICAN CRETACEOUS DINOSAURS
From North Africa to South Africa, paleontologists have uncovered fossil remains of dinosaurs that lived during the Cretaceous.

NIGERSAURUS

Nigersaurus had 500 front teeth.

With powerful arms, claws, webbed feet, crocodile-like jaws, and a flat tail for swimming, Spinosaurus preyed on fish in North Africa.

SPINOSAURUS

Suchomimus's narrow, tooth-filled jaws show why its name means "crocodile-like."

PARALITITAN

Carcharodontosaurus, named after the great white shark (Carcharodon), was a top predator capable of hunting the gigantic sauropod Paralititan.

SUCHOMIMUS

CARCHARODONTOSAURUS

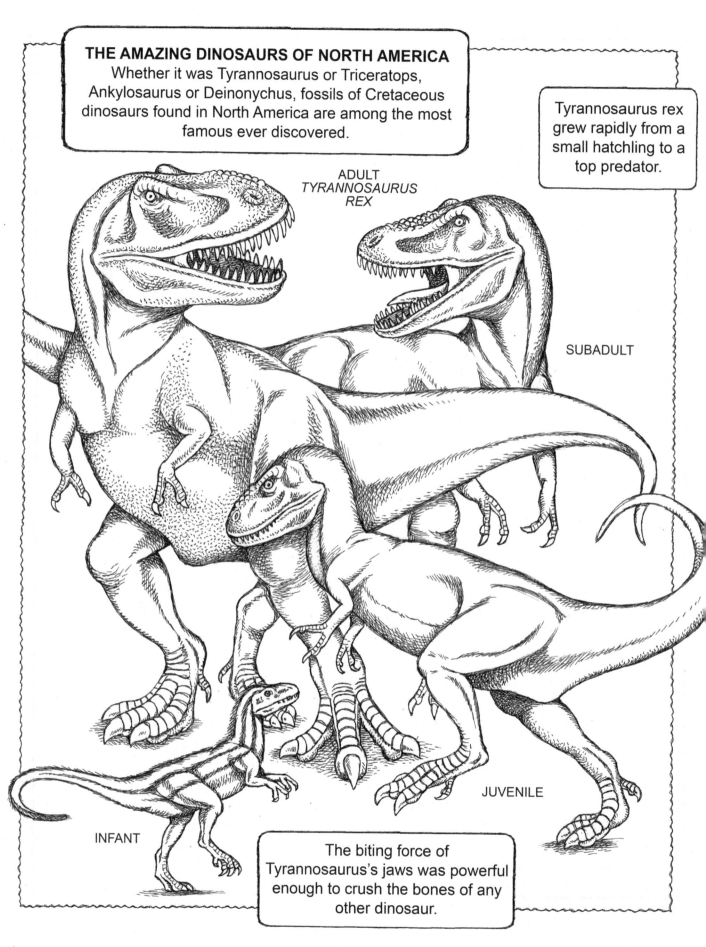

THE AMAZING DINOSAURS OF NORTH AMERICA
Whether it was Tyrannosaurus or Triceratops, Ankylosaurus or Deinonychus, fossils of Cretaceous dinosaurs found in North America are among the most famous ever discovered.

Tyrannosaurus rex grew rapidly from a small hatchling to a top predator.

ADULT
TYRANNOSAURUS REX

SUBADULT

JUVENILE

INFANT

The biting force of Tyrannosaurus's jaws was powerful enough to crush the bones of any other dinosaur.

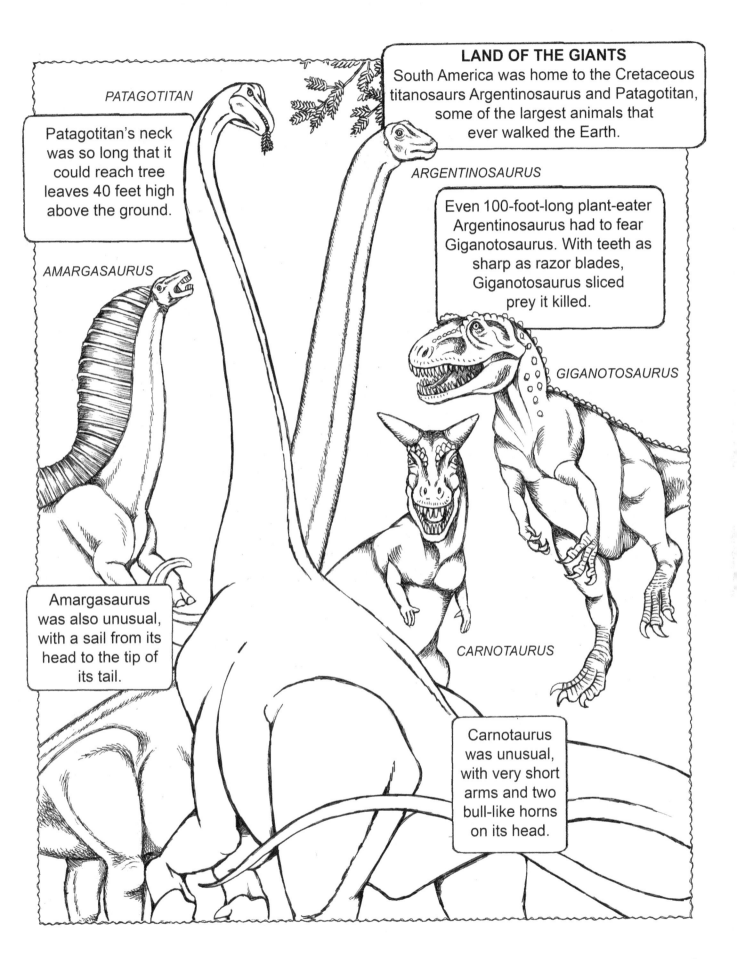

LAND OF THE GIANTS
South America was home to the Cretaceous titanosaurs Argentinosaurus and Patagotitan, some of the largest animals that ever walked the Earth.

PATAGOTITAN

Patagotitan's neck was so long that it could reach tree leaves 40 feet high above the ground.

ARGENTINOSAURUS

Even 100-foot-long plant-eater Argentinosaurus had to fear Giganotosaurus. With teeth as sharp as razor blades, Giganotosaurus sliced prey it killed.

AMARGASAURUS

GIGANOTOSAURUS

Amargasaurus was also unusual, with a sail from its head to the tip of its tail.

CARNOTAURUS

Carnotaurus was unusual, with very short arms and two bull-like horns on its head.

ASIA'S FEATHERED WONDERS

All of the fossils of feathered dinosaurs discovered in China and Mongolia have changed the ways in which paleontologists think about the evolution of dinosaurs and birds during the Cretaceous.

PSITTACOSAURUS

SHUVUUIA

Shuvuuia had three clawed toes in front and one behind, just like many birds.

ZHENYUANLONG

Which dinosaur had a beak like a parrot, walked on two legs, and grew stiff bristles on its tail? Psittacosaurus, of course.

Therizinosaurus may have used its three long claws to dig for beetles, ants, and other insects.

THERIZINOSAURUS

Though its name means "egg thief," there is no proof that Oviraptor ate dinosaur eggs. Like birds, it lacked teeth.

Although Zhenyuanlong's wing feathers were shaped like those of a bird's flight feathers, it could not fly.

One might mistake a galloping Caudipteryx for an ostrich, but it was a dinosaur.

SCANSORIOPTERYX

CAUDIPTERYX

Even though Scansoriopteryx couldn't fly, it probably used its long third finger to climb trees.

Don't be fooled by small, feathered Velociraptor. It was a fierce predator unafraid to attack Protoceratops with its slashing claws and sharp teeth.

VELOCIRAPTOR

PROTOCERATOPS

Like birds, the little dinosaur named Mei slept with her wing covering her head.

MEI

On pages 8, 12, 20, 22, 23, 33, 35, 36, 42, and 43 you will find ways in which dinosaurs and birds are similar. Most paleontologists are convinced that birds are living dinosaurs. Do you agree?

THE END OF THE AGE OF DINOSAURS
At the end of the Mesozoic, the last of the dinosaurs that walked the Earth died out. They became extinct, never to return again. The first clue to what happened was found in rocks.

Earth scientists found a thin layer of iridium in rocks dating 66 million years old. Iridium is rare on Earth's surface but common in asteroids whirling in outer space.

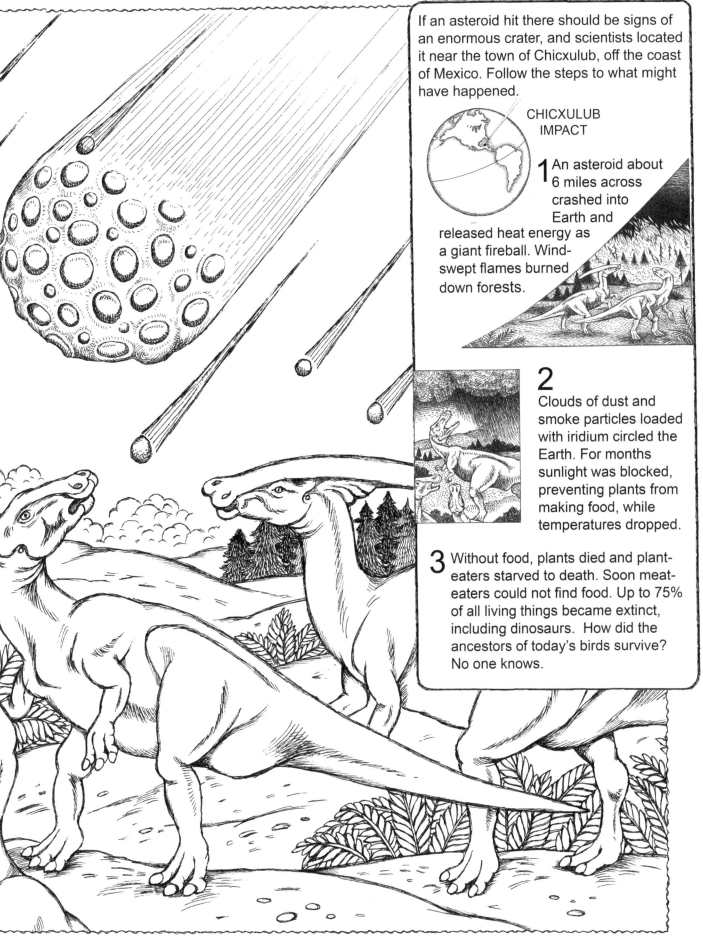

If an asteroid hit there should be signs of an enormous crater, and scientists located it near the town of Chicxulub, off the coast of Mexico. Follow the steps to what might have happened.

CHICXULUB IMPACT

1 An asteroid about 6 miles across crashed into Earth and released heat energy as a giant fireball. Wind-swept flames burned down forests.

2 Clouds of dust and smoke particles loaded with iridium circled the Earth. For months sunlight was blocked, preventing plants from making food, while temperatures dropped.

3 Without food, plants died and plant-eaters starved to death. Soon meat-eaters could not find food. Up to 75% of all living things became extinct, including dinosaurs. How did the ancestors of today's birds survive? No one knows.

VISIT A DINOSAUR
Around the world there are museums in which you can view dinosaur skeletons and other fossils. Take note of when and where each dinosaur lived and make drawings of skulls, claws, and other dinosaur parts.

Today, paleontologists use the latest scientific equipment to probe bones and other fossils to figure out how dinosaurs moved and bit into and chewed food, as well as what colors their feathers and eggs may have been.

If you can't get to a museum and are convinced birds are living dinosaurs, then just look up in the sky and wait for a dinosaur to fly by!

ORNITHISCHIANS